TRUCKS AND SUPERTRUCKS

TRUCKS and SUPERTRUCKS

NORMAN and PAT RICHARDS

DOUBLEDAY & COMPANY, INC., GARDEN CITY, NEW YORK

For Don Tefft and the loving memory of Opal Tefft of North East, Pennsylvania, with love and gratitude

This book is part of a Museum of Science and Industry/Chicago series of science books published by Doubleday & Company, Inc. The series is designed to inform, stimulate, and challenge youngsters on a wide range of scientific and technological subjects.

Library of Congress Cataloging in Publication Data

Richards, Norman.
   Trucks and supertrucks.

   SUMMARY: Describes the various kinds of tractor-trailer, dump, delivery, emergency, and recreational trucks and the functions they perform.
   1. Motor-trucks—Juvenile literature. [1. Trucks] I. Richards, Pat, joint author. II. Chicago. Museum of Science and Industry. III. Title.
TL230.R55   388.34'4
ISBN: 0-385-14069-x Trade
        0-385-14070-3 Prebound
Library of Congress Catalog Card Number 78–22350

CONTENTS

PREFACE

Trucks play a big role in our daily lives—perhaps more than we realize. Almost everything we buy in stores—our food, clothing, furniture, and hundreds of other items—is moved by truck. The lumber to build our homes, the oil and coal to heat them, the gasoline for the family car, all are delivered by truck.

The paper for this book began as logs in a forest. A truck carried the logs to a paper mill. Another truck hauled the paper to a printing plant. The chemicals and dyes in the ink were carried to the manufacturer in a tank truck; then the ink was delivered to the printer in a different truck. Finally, copies of the book were sent to book stores and libraries in trucks.

Even when things are shipped by train, boat, or airplane, trucks carry them the rest of the way to the customer. Two out of every three communities in the United States have no railroad service. And many more have no airport or boat harbor. Only trucks can deliver goods to every town and city.

That is why the business of moving things by truck is so important. More than nine million people work in the trucking industry in the United States. There are about twenty-nine million trucks in operation today, carrying almost every kind of product you can imagine.

There is a truck suited for every job. Some of them are the big tractor-trailer trucks you see on the highways, hauling heavy loads for long distances. Others are industrial trucks, carrying big loads of coal, sand, gravel or lumber, or mixing concrete for builders. Still others are small delivery trucks, bringing thousands of things to homes, stores, and offices.

This book shows some of the wonderful variety of trucks at work—making our lives easier by bringing us the things we need and moving everything that must be moved.

N.R. and P.R.

Photo by Pat Richards

TRACTOR-TRAILER TRUCKS

These tractor-trailer trucks are carrying tons of food to supermarkets. They haul oranges from Florida, potatoes from Maine, breakfast cereal from Michigan, and many other foods from many other places. The front part of the truck is called the "tractor." The back part is called the "trailer." The tractor hooks onto the trailer and pulls it. The engines on some trucks have more than 400 horsepower. This is two or three times as much power as family cars have. Many trucks have diesel engines. The diesel is a special type of engine that uses less fuel than other types.

Photo by American Trucking Associations, Inc.

Some tractors even pull two trailers. This truck is carrying a load of freight in each trailer. The driver can unhook the back trailer and leave it in one city. Then he can pull the front trailer to another city, where a customer is waiting for the freight. Almost everything we buy in stores is shipped by trucks.

Photo by Pat Richards

This is what it looks like in the driver's seat of a big truck. The dials and switches curve around the driver in this one, so he can reach them easily. In many trucks, there is a bed behind the seat so one driver can sleep while another drives. They can take turns sleeping on a long trip, so they don't have to stop the truck.

Photo by Aero Mayflower Transit Company, Inc.

This truck is called a moving van. When a family moves to a new home, the truck can carry all their furniture, dishes, and other things in one load. Many of these trucks have padding on the walls, so the furniture won't be scratched during the trip. The truck usually arrives when the family is ready to move into the new home.

Photo by American Trucking Associations, Inc.

Today's powerful trucks can even carry several other big trucks, piggyback style. This is how new trucks are delivered from factories to dealers. Customers buy the trucks from the dealers.

Photo by Pat Richards

Small pickup trucks and cars are also carried to dealers in special trailers. Sometimes eight cars are carried in one load. This load has just arrived from the factory. The new cars are driven off the trailer on ramps. Then they are driven into the dealer's showroom so customers can see them and buy them.

Photo by Fruehauf Corporation

Trucks carry huge logs from the forest to a lumber mill, where they will be cut into boards. This trailer has no floor. The logs are held by big U-shaped beams at the front and back. Heavy steel chains keep the top logs from falling off.

Photo by Fruehauf Corporation

This bulk tank trailer carries several tons of flour from a grain mill to large bakeries. The flour will be used for baking bread. To unload the truck, the driver connects big hoses or pipes to holes in the bottom of the tank. The flour pours out through the holes and goes into a storage place.

Photo by Pat Richards

Flatbed trailers are designed to carry big loads, such as these concrete sewer pipes. The pipes are being hauled from a factory to a place where a new sewer is being built. Flatbed trailers have no sides because the things they carry are sometimes wider than the truck. Big chains keep the pipes from rolling off.

Photo by Fruehauf Corporation

This is called a drop-frame trailer because the floor is lower than those on other trailers. This one carries two big sailboats. Parts of the boats almost reach the low floor, but the tops of the boats are not too high to go under bridges. If another type of truck tried to haul these boats, the tops would be too high.

J.J. AND SONS, INC.

This trailer rides on air

Photo by Pat Richards

Trucks carry horses for thousands of miles in special trailers. This one has fifteen stalls with padded walls. The horses won't be hurt if they bump into the walls during the ride. Many racehorses travel from one track to another in these trucks. Drivers put food in the stalls so the horses can eat while they ride.

Photo by Exxon Corporation

DUMP TRUCKS

Does this truck look small? If you look again, you will see that the wheels are twice as big as the driver. This is a giant mining truck being loaded with coal at a mine. It can carry 170 tons of coal. This is as much as a railroad freight car! The truck is too heavy to drive on highways because it would crack the pavement. It is only used in mines, to haul coal to railroad cars.

Photo by Pat Richards

Dump trucks are used everywhere to carry sand, earth, and gravel. They haul these materials to places where people are building new houses, dams, and office buildings. The sand, earth, and gravel are used to fill in holes and change the shape of the land. To dump the load, the driver pulls a lever and the truck body tips up. The back door or "tailgate" swings open and the load falls out.

Photo by Fruehauf Corporation

Giant dump trailers are used when there is a big job to do. They can move many tons of sand or gravel in one load. A motor pushes the tall pole up and tips the whole trailer to dump the load. Even some of the wheels are lifted off the ground.

Photo by Pat Richards

Here is a concrete-mixer truck. It is delivering concrete to workers who are making a new office building. The big mixer tank is filled with sand, cement, and gravel. The smaller tank is filled with water. The water runs into the mixer tank through a pipe while the truck is traveling on the road. A motor turns the big tank over and over, like a spinning top on its side. When the truck arrives at the construction site, the concrete is ready to be poured out. It pours out of a chute and the workers use it to make walls and floors.

Photo by Pat Richards

DELIVERY TRUCKS

Some stores and office buildings have giant windows. These are too big to be carried in most trucks. Also, they must be carried carefully or they will break. When new windows are needed, they are delivered in special trucks such as this one. The windows stand up straight against the tall frames on the sides. Brackets hold the glass tightly against the frames so it won't bump and break.

Photo by Pat Richards

Garbage trucks are used everywhere to take people's trash away. Workers empty garbage into the back of this truck. Then a motor drives a big scoop down from the top. It pushes all the garbage into the front of the truck body, packing it tightly. This makes it possible for the truck to haul more garbage than if it were packed loosely.

Photo by Exxon Corporation

When a home is heated by an oil furnace, the oil is delivered in a tank truck. The big tank has several walls inside. They keep the oil from moving to one side of the truck when it is traveling. The truck is easier to drive because it is not too heavy on one side. The driver puts the hose into a pipe that goes to the tank in the basement. A motor pumps the oil through the hose and a meter tells how much oil is delivered.

Photo by Pat Richards

Trucks deliver bottles and cans full of soft drinks to stores. These trucks have separate compartments, just the right size to hold cases of bottles. The compartment walls keep the bottles from bouncing around and breaking while the truck is traveling.

Photo by Pat Richards

Light van trucks carry bread, rolls, pies, and cakes from bakeries to food stores. Trucks like these also deliver other food such as potato chips and milk to small stores and super-markets.

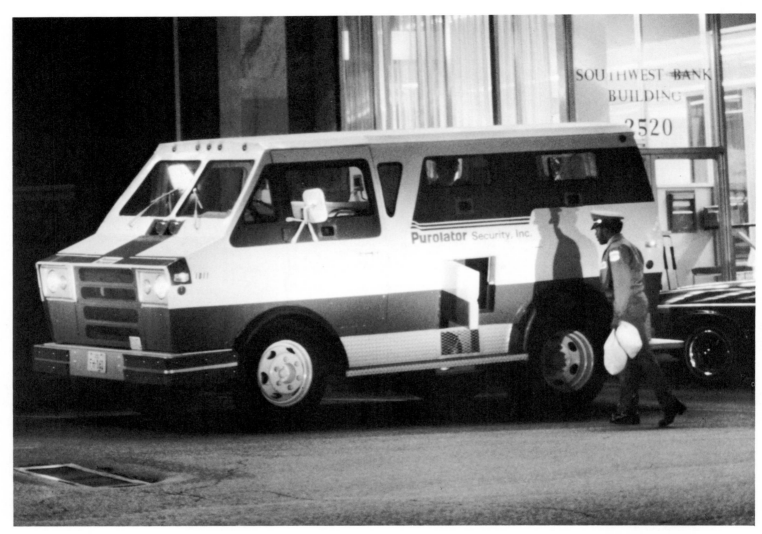

Photo by Purolator, Inc.

This small van is heavier than it looks. Its sides and top are covered with steel armor plating. It also has bulletproof windows, so a robber could not shoot the driver and guard inside. Armored trucks carry large sums of money from a bank's branch office to the main bank. The driver is putting bags of money into the truck through a special door that can only be opened from the inside. If robbers overpowered the driver outside the truck, they still could not reach the money and the armed guard locked inside.

Some trucks are designed to lift people and things into the air. This airport food truck is parked at the side door of a giant jet airliner. The airplane door is higher than the truck. So the truck body rises up to the level of the door, and workers can move the food into the plane.

Photo by Pat Richards

EMERGENCY TRUCKS

Look closely and you will see two men at the top of the electric-light pole, repairing some damaged wires. They don't have to climb the pole. Each truck has a "cherry picker." This is a long mechanical arm that rises up. It has a little box at the end. The man stands in the box and is lifted up to the electric wires so he can fix them.

Photo by Pat Richards

Sometimes firemen have to reach the tops of burning buildings to rescue people or put out a fire. Fire trucks such as this one have tall ladders for the firemen to climb. The part of the ladder at the front of the truck can be raised until the ladder is standing almost straight up. The truck has pumps to push water through hoses, so firemen can put out the fire. Many fire trucks carry water in tanks. They can also pump water from fire hydrants.

Photo by Pat Richards

Wrecker trucks have strong cranes and chains to lift the end of a car into the air. This makes it easier to pull a damaged car to a repair garage after an accident.

Photo by Pat Richards

RECREATIONAL TRUCKS

Many people like to make their pickup trucks into vacation campers. They buy a "camper" section to put into the truck body. It has beds to sleep in and a kitchen to eat in. The owners can take the camper section off the truck if they want to haul other loads.

59

Photo by Pat Richards

"Custom" vans are very popular, too. This van has the same body as a delivery truck, but big "picture windows" have been added. Inside, there are comfortable beds and tables. The owner can use it for weekend trips or on vacation.

Photo by Pat Richards

Children and grownups love to see trucks like this at playgrounds and beaches. The driver has a small stove in back where he can cook hot dogs and french fries. He also sells potato chips and cold drinks to hungry and thirsty people. At the end of the day, he closes his side window and drives home.

AUTHOR BIOGRAPHIES

Working as a husband-and-wife writer/photographer team, NORMAN and PAT RICHARDS often followed trucks on the spur of the moment to shoot many of the pictures in this book. "Trucks don't sit still for long," says Pat, the photographer, "so you have to catch them when and where you can."

NORMAN RICHARDS studied journalism at Boston University and did graduate work at Harvard University. He has been a magazine editor and writer for a number of years and has traveled throughout the world on assignments. He is the author of nineteen previous books on a wide variety of subjects.

PAT RICHARDS, a business-college graduate who has worked in advertising and magazine publishing, was formerly on the editorial staff of *Golf Digest* magazine. She has done photography for that organization and for publications in other fields.